50 Big Book of Doughnuts Recipes for Home

By: Kelly Johnson

Table of Contents

- Classic Glazed Doughnuts
- Chocolate Frosted Doughnuts
- Powdered Sugar Doughnuts
- Jelly-Filled Doughnuts
- Boston Cream Doughnuts
- Cinnamon Sugar Doughnuts
- Maple-Glazed Doughnuts
- Vanilla Sprinkle Doughnuts
- Double Chocolate Doughnuts
- Caramel Drizzle Doughnuts
- Old-Fashioned Sour Cream Doughnuts
- Blueberry Cake Doughnuts
- Pumpkin Spice Doughnuts
- Red Velvet Doughnuts
- Lemon Poppy Seed Doughnuts
- Strawberry Frosted Doughnuts
- Apple Cider Doughnuts
- S'mores Doughnuts
- Peanut Butter Glazed Doughnuts
- Matcha Green Tea Doughnuts
- Banana Bread Doughnuts
- Coconut Cream Doughnuts
- Honey-Glazed Doughnuts
- Churro Doughnuts
- Almond Crunch Doughnuts
- Orange Zest Doughnuts
- White Chocolate Raspberry Doughnuts
- Salted Caramel Doughnuts
- Mocha Glazed Doughnuts
- Gingerbread Doughnuts
- Pistachio Glazed Doughnuts
- Funfetti Doughnuts
- Raspberry Jam Doughnuts
- Tiramisu Doughnuts
- Mango Glazed Doughnuts

- Hazelnut Chocolate Doughnuts
- Cookies and Cream Doughnuts
- Butter Pecan Doughnuts
- Espresso Glazed Doughnuts
- Pineapple Upside-Down Doughnuts
- Lemon Blueberry Doughnuts
- Peanut Butter and Jelly Doughnuts
- Spiced Chai Doughnuts
- Maple Bacon Doughnuts
- Chocolate Chip Doughnuts
- Chocolate Coconut Doughnuts
- Mint Chocolate Doughnuts
- Strawberry Shortcake Doughnuts
- Key Lime Pie Doughnuts
- Black Forest Doughnuts

Classic Glazed Doughnuts

Ingredients

For the Doughnuts:

- 2 1/4 tsp (1 packet) active dry yeast
- 1/4 cup warm water (110°F/45°C)
- 3/4 cup whole milk, warmed
- 1/4 cup granulated sugar
- 1/2 tsp salt
- 1/4 cup unsalted butter, melted
- 2 large eggs
- 4 cups all-purpose flour
- Vegetable oil (for frying)

For the Glaze:

- 2 cups powdered sugar
- 1/4 cup whole milk
- 1 tsp vanilla extract

Instructions

1. Make the Dough:
In a bowl, combine the warm water and yeast. Let it sit for 5-10 minutes until foamy. In a large mixing bowl, whisk the milk, sugar, salt, melted butter, and eggs. Add the yeast mixture. Gradually stir in the flour until a soft dough forms. Transfer the dough to a lightly floured surface and knead for 5-7 minutes until smooth and elastic. Place the dough in a greased bowl, cover with a damp cloth, and let it rise for 1-2 hours until doubled in size.

2. Shape the Doughnuts:
Roll the dough out to about 1/2-inch thickness. Use a 3-inch round cutter (or a glass) to cut out circles. For the hole, use a 1-inch cutter (or bottle cap). Place the doughnuts and holes on a parchment-lined baking sheet. Cover and let rise for another 30 minutes.

3. Fry the Doughnuts:
Heat vegetable oil in a deep pot to 350°F (175°C). Fry the doughnuts in small batches for 1-2 minutes per side until golden brown. Remove with a slotted spoon and transfer to a paper towel-lined plate to drain.

4. Make the Glaze:
In a bowl, whisk together powdered sugar, milk, and vanilla until smooth. Dip the warm doughnuts into the glaze, covering them evenly. Place them on a wire rack to set.

Chocolate Frosted Doughnuts

Ingredients:
For the Doughnuts:

- 2 1/4 tsp active dry yeast
- 1/4 cup warm water (110°F/45°C)
- 3/4 cup whole milk, warmed
- 1/4 cup granulated sugar
- 1/2 tsp salt
- 1/4 cup unsalted butter, melted
- 2 large eggs
- 4 cups all-purpose flour
- Vegetable oil (for frying)
  For the Chocolate Frosting:
- 1 cup powdered sugar
- 1/4 cup cocoa powder
- 3 tbsp milk
- 1/2 tsp vanilla extract
- Sprinkles (optional)

Instructions:
Make the dough by mixing the yeast and water, allowing it to foam. Whisk milk, sugar, salt, butter, and eggs in a large bowl. Add yeast mixture and flour, knead, and let rise for 1-2 hours. Roll and cut into circles, then let rise again for 30 minutes. Fry the doughnuts at 350°F until golden. For the frosting, mix powdered sugar, cocoa, milk, and vanilla. Dip warm doughnuts into frosting and top with sprinkles.

Powdered Sugar Doughnuts

Ingredients:

For the Doughnuts:

- 2 1/4 tsp active dry yeast
- 1/4 cup warm water
- 3/4 cup warm whole milk
- 1/4 cup granulated sugar
- 1/2 tsp salt
- 1/4 cup melted unsalted butter
- 2 eggs
- 4 cups all-purpose flour
- Vegetable oil (for frying)
  For Coating:
- 2 cups powdered sugar

Instructions:

Make the dough using the same method as above. After frying the doughnuts at 350°F, let them cool slightly. While still warm, toss the doughnuts in a bowl of powdered sugar until evenly coated.

Jelly-Filled Doughnuts

Ingredients:

For the Doughnuts:

- 2 1/4 tsp active dry yeast
- 1/4 cup warm water
- 3/4 cup warm milk
- 1/4 cup sugar
- 1/2 tsp salt
- 1/4 cup unsalted butter, melted
- 2 eggs
- 4 cups all-purpose flour
- Vegetable oil (for frying)
  For Filling and Dusting:
- 1 cup raspberry or strawberry jam
- 2 cups powdered sugar

Instructions:

Prepare the dough as described earlier. After frying the doughnuts, let them cool. Use a pastry bag with a small tip to pipe jam into the center of each doughnut. Roll the filled doughnuts in powdered sugar for a sweet finish.

Boston Cream Doughnuts

Ingredients:

For the Doughnuts:

- 2 1/4 tsp active dry yeast
- 1/4 cup warm water
- 3/4 cup warm milk
- 1/4 cup sugar
- 1/2 tsp salt
- 1/4 cup melted butter
- 2 eggs
- 4 cups all-purpose flour
- Vegetable oil (for frying)

  For the Filling:
- 2 cups pastry cream

  For the Chocolate Glaze:
- 1 cup semi-sweet chocolate chips
- 1/2 cup heavy cream

Instructions:

Prepare the doughnuts as usual. After frying, fill each with pastry cream using a pastry bag. For the glaze, melt chocolate chips and heavy cream. Dip the top of each doughnut into the glaze and let it set.

Cinnamon Sugar Doughnuts

Ingredients:

For the Doughnuts:

- 2 1/4 tsp active dry yeast
- 1/4 cup warm water
- 3/4 cup warm milk
- 1/4 cup sugar
- 1/2 tsp salt
- 1/4 cup melted butter
- 2 eggs
- 4 cups all-purpose flour
- Vegetable oil (for frying)
  For Coating:
- 1 cup granulated sugar
- 2 tsp ground cinnamon

Instructions:

Prepare and fry the doughnuts. While still warm, toss them in a mix of cinnamon and sugar until evenly coated.

Maple-Glazed Doughnuts

Ingredients:

For the Doughnuts:

- 2 1/4 tsp active dry yeast
- 1/4 cup warm water
- 3/4 cup warm milk
- 1/4 cup sugar
- 1/2 tsp salt
- 1/4 cup melted butter
- 2 eggs
- 4 cups all-purpose flour
- Vegetable oil (for frying)
  For the Maple Glaze:
- 1 cup powdered sugar
- 1/4 cup maple syrup
- 2 tbsp milk

Instructions:

After frying the doughnuts, whisk together the glaze ingredients. Dip the tops of each doughnut in the glaze and let them set.

Vanilla Sprinkle Doughnuts

Ingredients:
For the Doughnuts:

- 2 1/4 tsp active dry yeast
- 1/4 cup warm water
- 3/4 cup warm milk
- 1/4 cup sugar
- 1/2 tsp salt
- 1/4 cup melted butter
- 2 eggs
- 4 cups all-purpose flour
- Vegetable oil (for frying)
  For the Glaze:
- 1 cup powdered sugar
- 3 tbsp milk
- 1 tsp vanilla extract
- Sprinkles

Instructions:
Prepare the dough and fry. Mix powdered sugar, milk, and vanilla for the glaze. Dip each doughnut and top with sprinkles before the glaze sets.

Double Chocolate Doughnuts

Ingredients:

For the Doughnuts:

- 1 1/2 cups all-purpose flour
- 1/2 cup cocoa powder
- 1 tsp baking powder
- 1/2 tsp baking soda
- 1/4 tsp salt
- 1/2 cup sugar
- 2 eggs
- 1/2 cup milk
- 1/4 cup vegetable oil

For the Glaze:

- 1 cup powdered sugar
- 1/4 cup cocoa powder
- 3 tbsp milk

Instructions:

Mix dry and wet ingredients separately, then combine. Bake in doughnut molds at 350°F for 12-15 minutes. Dip cooled doughnuts in chocolate glaze.

Caramel Drizzle Doughnuts

Ingredients:
For the Doughnuts:

- 2 1/4 tsp active dry yeast
- 1/4 cup warm water
- 3/4 cup warm milk
- 1/4 cup sugar
- 1/2 tsp salt
- 1/4 cup melted butter
- 2 eggs
- 4 cups all-purpose flour
- Vegetable oil (for frying)
  For the Caramel Sauce:
- 1/2 cup sugar
- 2 tbsp butter
- 1/4 cup heavy cream

Instructions:
Fry the doughnuts. For the caramel, melt sugar until golden, then stir in butter and cream. Drizzle the caramel over the doughnuts.

Old-Fashioned Sour Cream Doughnuts

Ingredients:

- 2 1/4 cups all-purpose flour
- 1 tsp baking powder
- 1/2 tsp baking soda
- 1/4 tsp salt
- 1/2 cup sugar
- 2 eggs
- 1/2 cup sour cream
- 1/4 cup melted butter
- Vegetable oil (for frying)

Instructions:

Mix dry and wet ingredients separately, then combine. Roll out dough, cut shapes, and fry at 350°F until golden.

Blueberry Cake Doughnuts

Ingredients:

- 2 1/4 cups all-purpose flour
- 1/2 cup sugar
- 1 tsp baking powder
- 1/2 tsp baking soda
- 1/4 tsp salt
- 1/2 cup milk
- 1/4 cup melted butter
- 2 eggs
- 1/2 cup fresh blueberries

Instructions:

Mix dry ingredients, then add wet ingredients and blueberries. Bake in doughnut molds at 350°F for 12-15 minutes.

Pumpkin Spice Doughnuts

Ingredients:

- 2 cups all-purpose flour
- 1/2 cup sugar
- 1 tsp baking powder
- 1/2 tsp baking soda
- 1/4 tsp salt
- 2 tsp pumpkin pie spice
- 2 eggs
- 1/2 cup pumpkin puree
- 1/4 cup melted butter
- 1/4 cup milk

Instructions:
Mix dry and wet ingredients separately, then combine. Bake in doughnut molds at 350°F for 12-15 minutes. Optionally, dust with cinnamon sugar after baking.

Red Velvet Doughnuts

Ingredients:

- 2 cups all-purpose flour
- 1/2 cup sugar
- 2 tbsp cocoa powder
- 1 tsp baking powder
- 1/2 tsp baking soda
- 1/4 tsp salt
- 2 eggs
- 1/2 cup buttermilk
- 1/4 cup vegetable oil
- 1 tsp red food coloring

Instructions:
Mix dry and wet ingredients separately, then combine. Bake in doughnut molds at 350°F for 12-15 minutes. Optionally, top with cream cheese glaze.

Lemon Poppy Seed Doughnuts

Ingredients:

- 2 cups all-purpose flour
- 1/2 cup sugar
- 1 tsp baking powder
- 1/2 tsp baking soda
- 1/4 tsp salt
- 1 tbsp poppy seeds
- 2 eggs
- 1/2 cup milk
- 1/4 cup melted butter
- 2 tbsp lemon juice
- Zest of 1 lemon

Instructions:

Combine dry and wet ingredients, then mix. Bake in doughnut molds at 350°F for 12-15 minutes. Drizzle with lemon glaze if desired.

Strawberry Frosted Doughnuts

Ingredients:

For the Doughnuts:

- 2 cups all-purpose flour
- 1/2 cup sugar
- 1 tsp baking powder
- 1/2 tsp baking soda
- 1/4 tsp salt
- 2 eggs
- 1/2 cup milk
- 1/4 cup vegetable oil
  For the Frosting:
- 1 cup powdered sugar
- 2 tbsp strawberry puree
- 1 tbsp milk
- Sprinkles (optional)

Instructions:

Prepare and bake doughnuts. For the frosting, mix powdered sugar, puree, and milk. Dip doughnuts and decorate with sprinkles.

Apple Cider Doughnuts

Ingredients:

- 2 1/4 cups all-purpose flour
- 1/2 cup sugar
- 1 tsp baking powder
- 1/2 tsp baking soda
- 1/4 tsp salt
- 1 tsp cinnamon
- 1/2 cup apple cider
- 1/4 cup melted butter
- 2 eggs

Instructions:
Combine dry and wet ingredients, then mix. Fry or bake the doughnuts and coat in cinnamon sugar while warm.

S'mores Doughnuts

Ingredients:

- 2 cups all-purpose flour
- 1/2 cup sugar
- 1 tsp baking powder
- 1/4 tsp salt
- 2 eggs
- 1/2 cup milk
- 1/4 cup vegetable oil
  For the Topping:
- 1/2 cup melted chocolate
- 1/4 cup crushed graham crackers
- Mini marshmallows

Instructions:
Bake doughnuts, dip in melted chocolate, and top with graham cracker crumbs and mini marshmallows. Toast marshmallows if desired.

Peanut Butter Glazed Doughnuts

Ingredients:

For the Doughnuts:

- 2 cups all-purpose flour
- 1/2 cup sugar
- 1 tsp baking powder
- 1/2 tsp baking soda
- 1/4 tsp salt
- 2 eggs
- 1/2 cup milk
- 1/4 cup vegetable oil
  For the Glaze:
- 1/2 cup peanut butter
- 1 cup powdered sugar
- 2-3 tbsp milk

Instructions:

Prepare doughnuts and bake. For the glaze, mix peanut butter, powdered sugar, and milk. Dip doughnuts into glaze and let set.

Matcha Green Tea Doughnuts

Ingredients:

For the Doughnuts:

- 2 cups all-purpose flour
- 1/2 cup sugar
- 1 tsp baking powder
- 1/4 tsp salt
- 2 eggs
- 1/2 cup milk
- 1/4 cup vegetable oil

For the Glaze:

- 1 cup powdered sugar
- 1-2 tsp matcha powder
- 2-3 tbsp milk

Instructions:

Bake doughnuts, then prepare glaze by whisking powdered sugar, matcha, and milk. Dip doughnuts into glaze and let them set.

Banana Bread Doughnuts

Ingredients:

- 2 cups all-purpose flour
- 1 tsp baking powder
- 1/2 tsp baking soda
- 1/4 tsp salt
- 1/2 tsp cinnamon
- 1/2 cup sugar
- 2 ripe bananas, mashed
- 2 eggs
- 1/4 cup melted butter
- 1/2 cup milk

Instructions:
Mix dry ingredients in one bowl and wet ingredients in another. Combine the two and mix until just combined. Bake in doughnut molds at 350°F for 12-15 minutes. Optionally, top with a glaze or powdered sugar.

Coconut Cream Doughnuts

Ingredients:

- 2 cups all-purpose flour
- 1/2 cup sugar
- 1 tsp baking powder
- 1/2 tsp baking soda
- 1/4 tsp salt
- 2 eggs
- 1/2 cup coconut milk
- 1/4 cup melted butter
- 1/2 cup shredded coconut

Instructions:
Combine dry and wet ingredients separately, then mix. Fold in shredded coconut and bake in doughnut molds at 350°F for 12-15 minutes. Top with a coconut glaze if desired.

Honey-Glazed Doughnuts

Ingredients:
For the Doughnuts:

- 2 1/4 cups all-purpose flour
- 1/2 cup sugar
- 1 tsp baking powder
- 1/2 tsp baking soda
- 1/4 tsp salt
- 2 eggs
- 1/2 cup milk
- 1/4 cup vegetable oil

For the Glaze:

- 1/2 cup honey
- 1/4 cup powdered sugar
- 1-2 tbsp milk

Instructions:
Bake the doughnuts. For the glaze, mix honey, powdered sugar, and milk. Dip warm doughnuts in the glaze and let set.

Churro Doughnuts

Ingredients:

For the Doughnuts:

- 2 cups all-purpose flour
- 1/2 cup sugar
- 1 tsp baking powder
- 1/2 tsp baking soda
- 1/4 tsp salt
- 2 eggs
- 1/2 cup milk
- 1/4 cup vegetable oil

For Coating:

- 1 cup sugar
- 2 tsp cinnamon

Instructions:

Bake doughnuts and let them cool. Mix sugar and cinnamon, then roll the doughnuts in the mixture until coated.

Almond Crunch Doughnuts

Ingredients:

- 2 cups all-purpose flour
- 1/2 cup sugar
- 1 tsp baking powder
- 1/2 tsp baking soda
- 1/4 tsp salt
- 2 eggs
- 1/2 cup milk
- 1/4 cup vegetable oil
- 1/2 cup sliced almonds

Instructions:

Prepare the batter by mixing dry and wet ingredients separately. Fold in sliced almonds before baking in molds at 350°F for 12-15 minutes. Optionally, top with almond glaze or additional almonds.

Orange Zest Doughnuts

Ingredients:

- 2 cups all-purpose flour
- 1/2 cup sugar
- 1 tsp baking powder
- 1/2 tsp baking soda
- 1/4 tsp salt
- 2 eggs
- 1/2 cup milk
- 1/4 cup vegetable oil
- Zest of 1 orange
- 2 tbsp orange juice

Instructions:
Mix dry and wet ingredients, incorporating orange zest and juice. Bake in doughnut molds at 350°F for 12-15 minutes. Optionally, drizzle with an orange glaze.

White Chocolate Raspberry Doughnuts

Ingredients:

- 2 cups all-purpose flour
- 1/2 cup sugar
- 1 tsp baking powder
- 1/2 tsp baking soda
- 1/4 tsp salt
- 2 eggs
- 1/2 cup milk
- 1/4 cup melted white chocolate
- 1/2 cup raspberries

Instructions:

Combine dry and wet ingredients, then gently fold in raspberries. Bake in molds at 350°F for 12-15 minutes. Drizzle with white chocolate glaze if desired.

Salted Caramel Doughnuts

Ingredients:

For the Doughnuts:

- 2 cups all-purpose flour
- 1/2 cup sugar
- 1 tsp baking powder
- 1/2 tsp baking soda
- 1/4 tsp salt
- 2 eggs
- 1/2 cup milk
- 1/4 cup vegetable oil

For the Salted Caramel Sauce:

- 1/2 cup sugar
- 2 tbsp butter
- 1/4 cup heavy cream
- Sea salt for sprinkling

Instructions:

Bake doughnuts and let cool. For the caramel, melt sugar until golden, then stir in butter and cream. Drizzle over doughnuts and sprinkle with sea salt.

Mocha Glazed Doughnuts

Ingredients:

- 2 cups all-purpose flour
- 1/2 cup sugar
- 1 tsp baking powder
- 1/2 tsp baking soda
- 1/4 tsp salt
- 2 eggs
- 1/2 cup milk
- 1/4 cup brewed coffee (cooled)
- 1/4 cup vegetable oil
- 2 tbsp cocoa powder

Instructions:
Combine dry ingredients in one bowl and wet ingredients in another. Mix and bake in doughnut molds at 350°F for 12-15 minutes. For the glaze, mix powdered sugar with brewed coffee and cocoa powder, then dip cooled doughnuts.

Gingerbread Doughnuts

Ingredients:

- 2 cups all-purpose flour
- 1/2 cup sugar
- 1 tsp baking powder
- 1/2 tsp baking soda
- 1/4 tsp salt
- 2 tsp ground ginger
- 1 tsp cinnamon
- 1/2 tsp nutmeg
- 1/4 cup molasses
- 2 eggs
- 1/2 cup milk
- 1/4 cup vegetable oil

Instructions:
Mix dry and wet ingredients separately. Combine and bake in doughnut molds at 350°F for 12-15 minutes. Optionally, drizzle with a glaze made of powdered sugar and milk.

Pistachio Glazed Doughnuts

Ingredients:

- 2 cups all-purpose flour
- 1/2 cup sugar
- 1 tsp baking powder
- 1/2 tsp baking soda
- 1/4 tsp salt
- 2 eggs
- 1/2 cup milk
- 1/4 cup vegetable oil
- 1/2 cup ground pistachios

Instructions:

Combine dry and wet ingredients, then mix. Bake in doughnut molds at 350°F for 12-15 minutes. For the glaze, mix powdered sugar with milk and ground pistachios, then dip cooled doughnuts.

Funfetti Doughnuts

Ingredients:

- 2 cups all-purpose flour
- 1/2 cup sugar
- 1 tsp baking powder
- 1/2 tsp baking soda
- 1/4 tsp salt
- 2 eggs
- 1/2 cup milk
- 1/4 cup vegetable oil
- 1/2 cup rainbow sprinkles

Instructions:

Mix dry and wet ingredients separately, then fold in sprinkles. Bake in doughnut molds at 350°F for 12-15 minutes. Top with a simple glaze or more sprinkles if desired.

Raspberry Jam Doughnuts

Ingredients:

- 2 cups all-purpose flour
- 1/2 cup sugar
- 1 tsp baking powder
- 1/2 tsp baking soda
- 1/4 tsp salt
- 2 eggs
- 1/2 cup milk
- 1/4 cup vegetable oil
- 1/2 cup raspberry jam

Instructions:

Prepare the batter by mixing dry and wet ingredients. Fill doughnut molds halfway, add a teaspoon of jam in the center, then cover with more batter. Bake at 350°F for 12-15 minutes. Dust with powdered sugar after cooling.

Tiramisu Doughnuts

Ingredients:

- 2 cups all-purpose flour
- 1/2 cup sugar
- 1 tsp baking powder
- 1/2 tsp baking soda
- 1/4 tsp salt
- 2 eggs
- 1/2 cup milk
- 1/4 cup brewed espresso (cooled)
- 1/4 cup mascarpone cheese

Instructions:
Combine dry and wet ingredients separately, then mix until smooth. Bake in doughnut molds at 350°F for 12-15 minutes. For the glaze, mix powdered sugar with espresso and dip cooled doughnuts, then dust with cocoa powder.

Mango Glazed Doughnuts

Ingredients:

- 2 cups all-purpose flour
- 1/2 cup sugar
- 1 tsp baking powder
- 1/2 tsp baking soda
- 1/4 tsp salt
- 2 eggs
- 1/2 cup milk
- 1/4 cup vegetable oil
- 1/2 cup mango puree

Instructions:

Mix dry and wet ingredients separately, then combine. Bake in doughnut molds at 350°F for 12-15 minutes. For the glaze, mix powdered sugar with mango puree and dip cooled doughnuts.

Hazelnut Chocolate Doughnuts

Ingredients:

- 2 cups all-purpose flour
- 1/2 cup sugar
- 1 tsp baking powder
- 1/2 tsp baking soda
- 1/4 tsp salt
- 2 eggs
- 1/2 cup milk
- 1/4 cup hazelnut spread
- 1/4 cup vegetable oil
- 1/2 cup chopped hazelnuts

Instructions:
Prepare the batter by mixing dry and wet ingredients. Fold in chopped hazelnuts and bake in molds at 350°F for 12-15 minutes. For the glaze, mix powdered sugar with milk and drizzle over cooled doughnuts.

Cookies and Cream Doughnuts

Ingredients:

- 2 cups all-purpose flour
- 1/2 cup sugar
- 1 tsp baking powder
- 1/2 tsp baking soda
- 1/4 tsp salt
- 2 eggs
- 1/2 cup milk
- 1/4 cup vegetable oil
- 1/2 cup crushed chocolate sandwich cookies

Instructions:

Mix dry and wet ingredients separately, then fold in crushed cookies. Bake in doughnut molds at 350°F for 12-15 minutes. For the glaze, mix powdered sugar with milk and more crushed cookies, then dip cooled doughnuts.

Butter Pecan Doughnuts

Ingredients:

- 2 cups all-purpose flour
- 1/2 cup sugar
- 1 tsp baking powder
- 1/2 tsp baking soda
- 1/4 tsp salt
- 2 eggs
- 1/2 cup milk
- 1/4 cup melted butter
- 1/2 cup chopped pecans

Instructions:
Combine dry and wet ingredients separately, then fold in chopped pecans. Bake in doughnut molds at 350°F for 12-15 minutes. For the glaze, mix powdered sugar with milk and melted butter, then dip cooled doughnuts.

Espresso Glazed Doughnuts

Ingredients:

- 2 cups all-purpose flour
- 1/2 cup sugar
- 1 tsp baking powder
- 1/2 tsp baking soda
- 1/4 tsp salt
- 2 eggs
- 1/2 cup milk
- 1/4 cup brewed espresso (cooled)

Instructions:

Mix dry and wet ingredients separately. Combine and bake in doughnut molds at 350°F for 12-15 minutes. For the glaze, mix powdered sugar with cooled espresso and dip cooled doughnuts.

Pineapple Upside-Down Doughnuts

Ingredients:

- 2 cups all-purpose flour
- 1/2 cup sugar
- 1 tsp baking powder
- 1/2 tsp baking soda
- 1/4 tsp salt
- 2 eggs
- 1/2 cup milk
- 1/4 cup vegetable oil
- 1/2 cup crushed pineapple, drained
- Maraschino cherries (for topping)

Instructions:
Prepare the batter by mixing dry and wet ingredients. Fold in crushed pineapple and pour into molds. Place a cherry in the center of each doughnut and bake at 350°F for 12-15 minutes.

Lemon Blueberry Doughnuts

Ingredients:

- 2 cups all-purpose flour
- 1/2 cup sugar
- 1 tsp baking powder
- 1/2 tsp baking soda
- 1/4 tsp salt
- 2 eggs
- 1/2 cup milk
- 1/4 cup vegetable oil
- Zest of 1 lemon
- 1/2 cup fresh blueberries

Instructions:
Combine dry and wet ingredients separately, then fold in lemon zest and blueberries. Bake in doughnut molds at 350°F for 12-15 minutes. For the glaze, mix powdered sugar with lemon juice and dip cooled doughnuts.

Peanut Butter and Jelly Doughnuts

Ingredients:

- 2 cups all-purpose flour
- 1/2 cup sugar
- 1 tsp baking powder
- 1/2 tsp baking soda
- 1/4 tsp salt
- 2 eggs
- 1/2 cup milk
- 1/4 cup peanut butter
- 1/2 cup raspberry or strawberry jam

Instructions:

Prepare the batter by mixing dry and wet ingredients. Fill doughnut molds halfway, add a teaspoon of jam in the center, then cover with more batter. Bake at 350°F for 12-15 minutes. Dust with powdered sugar after cooling.

Spiced Chai Doughnuts

Ingredients:

- 2 cups all-purpose flour
- 1/2 cup sugar
- 1 tsp baking powder
- 1/2 tsp baking soda
- 1/4 tsp salt
- 2 eggs
- 1/2 cup milk
- 1/4 cup vegetable oil
- 1 tsp chai spice blend

Instructions:

Mix dry and wet ingredients separately. Combine and bake in doughnut molds at 350°F for 12-15 minutes. For the glaze, mix powdered sugar with milk and chai spice, then dip cooled doughnuts.

Maple Bacon Doughnuts

Ingredients:

- 2 cups all-purpose flour
- 1/2 cup sugar
- 1 tsp baking powder
- 1/2 tsp baking soda
- 1/4 tsp salt
- 2 eggs
- 1/2 cup milk
- 1/4 cup maple syrup
- 1/2 cup cooked and crumbled bacon

Instructions:

Prepare the batter by mixing dry and wet ingredients separately. Fold in crumbled bacon and bake in doughnut molds at 350°F for 12-15 minutes. For the glaze, mix powdered sugar with maple syrup and dip cooled doughnuts.

Chocolate Chip Doughnuts

Ingredients:

- 2 cups all-purpose flour
- 1/2 cup sugar
- 1 tsp baking powder
- 1/2 tsp baking soda
- 1/4 tsp salt
- 2 eggs
- 1/2 cup milk
- 1/4 cup vegetable oil
- 1/2 cup chocolate chips

Instructions:
Combine dry and wet ingredients separately, then fold in chocolate chips. Bake in doughnut molds at 350°F for 12-15 minutes. For the glaze, mix powdered sugar with milk and drizzle over cooled doughnuts.

Chocolate Coconut Doughnuts

Ingredients:

- 2 cups all-purpose flour
- 1/2 cup sugar
- 1 tsp baking powder
- 1/2 tsp baking soda
- 1/4 tsp salt
- 2 eggs
- 1/2 cup milk
- 1/4 cup vegetable oil
- 1/2 cup unsweetened cocoa powder
- 1/2 cup shredded coconut

Instructions:

Mix dry and wet ingredients separately. Combine and fold in shredded coconut. Bake in doughnut molds at 350°F for 12-15 minutes. For the glaze, mix powdered sugar with coconut milk and dip cooled doughnuts in shredded coconut.

Mint Chocolate Doughnuts

Ingredients:

- 2 cups all-purpose flour
- 1/2 cup sugar
- 1 tsp baking powder
- 1/2 tsp baking soda
- 1/4 tsp salt
- 2 eggs
- 1/2 cup milk
- 1/4 cup vegetable oil
- 1/2 cup unsweetened cocoa powder
- 1/2 tsp peppermint extract

Instructions:

Prepare the batter by mixing dry and wet ingredients separately, adding peppermint extract to the wet mix. Bake in doughnut molds at 350°F for 12-15 minutes. For the glaze, mix powdered sugar with milk and peppermint extract, then dip cooled doughnuts.

Strawberry Shortcake Doughnuts

Ingredients:

- 2 cups all-purpose flour
- 1/2 cup sugar
- 1 tsp baking powder
- 1/2 tsp baking soda
- 1/4 tsp salt
- 2 eggs
- 1/2 cup milk
- 1/4 cup vegetable oil
- 1 cup diced fresh strawberries
- Whipped cream (for topping)

Instructions:

Combine dry and wet ingredients separately, then fold in diced strawberries. Bake in doughnut molds at 350°F for 12-15 minutes. Once cooled, top with whipped cream and more strawberries.

Key Lime Pie Doughnuts

Ingredients:

- 2 cups all-purpose flour
- 1/2 cup sugar
- 1 tsp baking powder
- 1/2 tsp baking soda
- 1/4 tsp salt
- 2 eggs
- 1/2 cup milk
- 1/4 cup vegetable oil
- Zest and juice of 2 key limes
- 1/2 cup crushed graham crackers (for topping)

Instructions:

Mix dry and wet ingredients separately, incorporating key lime zest and juice into the wet mixture. Bake in doughnut molds at 350°F for 12-15 minutes. For the glaze, mix powdered sugar with key lime juice and dip cooled doughnuts, then sprinkle with crushed graham crackers.

Black Forest Doughnuts

Ingredients:

- 2 cups all-purpose flour
- 1/2 cup sugar
- 1 tsp baking powder
- 1/2 tsp baking soda
- 1/4 tsp salt
- 2 eggs
- 1/2 cup milk
- 1/4 cup vegetable oil
- 1/2 cup unsweetened cocoa powder
- 1/2 cup cherry pie filling
- Whipped cream (for topping)

Instructions:
Combine dry and wet ingredients separately, then fold in cocoa powder. Bake in doughnut molds at 350°F for 12-15 minutes. Once cooled, fill each doughnut with cherry pie filling and top with whipped cream.

www.ingramcontent.com/pod-product-compliance
Lightning Source LLC
LaVergne TN
LVHW061950070526
838199LV00060B/4058